FOLLOW IT THROUGH
Writing in Context

Donn Byrne
and
Susan Holden

Longman

1. September

①

Jenny returns to the flat after a long day at college. Judy is waiting to go out.
Look at the photographs of the characters on pages 63 and 64, and read about them,
before you begin these exercises.

JENNY: God, I'm tired! That place is absolutely impossible!

JUDY: Oh, cheer up! The first week's always the worst. Anyway, you didn't
come here for a holiday. I mean, you *are* doing a secretarial course.

JENNY: Yes, but they give us so much work . . . And now they've lost my
registration form, so I've got to fill in another one – by tomorrow
morning!

JUDY: Oh, just stop grumbling and get on with it. Anyway, I've got to go now,
otherwise I'll be late. David's play starts at eight.

JENNY: Nicholas is asleep, then, is he?

JUDY: Yes. He probably won't wake up till we get back – if you're lucky!
Oh, by the way, there's a letter from Mum for you.

JENNY: Oh, thanks. See you later, then.

JUDY: Bye.
(*Judy goes out.*)

Miss Jenny Anderson,
Flat B,
16 Upper Street,
LONDON N1B 5BX.

Jenny sits down and reads her mother's letter.

18 Craigmillar Road, Edinburgh EG6 7YY
Tel: 031 556 1342

12 September

Dear Jenny,

I hope you've settled down after your first few days in London.
I know it's not easy, sharing a small flat with other people,
but do try and be nice to Judy. She has enough problems with a
small baby. And David <u>still</u> hasn't got a good job!
Your father's very busy at the moment planning another trip to
Europe. He'll probably be away about a month this time. He's
not quite sure which countries he'll have to go to, but it will
probably include France and Holland. And of course he hopes to
go to Italy, so that he can see Louise (by the way, don't forget
to write to her!).
Steve's the same as ever. His pop group's going well. In fact,
they're giving a concert quite soon. I just wish he'd work a bit
harder at school!
I really enjoy my new job at the hospital - you meet all sorts of
people. You could write quite a book about them!
Well, that's all for now. What's college like? Write and tell
us all about it. We're longing to hear!

Much love,

Mum.

P.S. Love to Judy and David too. And
Nicholas, of course!

2b

Jenny decides to fill in the college registration form first. Use suitable information from this unit and from the biographical data on pages 63 and 64 to complete it. Invent any details you do not know.

```
VICTORIA LANGUAGE AND SECRETARIAL COLLEGE,
25 VICTORIA STREET,  LONDON SW1B  8HJ



Registration form for secretarial courses.

FAMILY NAME..................... FIRST NAME(S)............
LONDON ADDRESS............................................
.........................................................
DATE OF BIRTH......................... TEL.NO.359.0507
NAME AND ADDRESS OF PARENT OR GUARDIAN....................
.........................................................
HAVE YOU EVER HAD SECRETARIAL TRAINING BEFORE? (YES/NO)....
IF SO, GIVE DETAILS.......................................
WHAT LANGUAGES DO YOU SPEAK? .............................
WHERE DID YOU STUDY THEM? ................................
INTERESTS AND HOBBIES.....................................
```

2c

To cheer herself up, Jenny decides to write to her boyfriend, Andrew. Complete her letter.

Flat B,
_____

14th. September.

Darling Andrew,
   Why haven't you written! I expected _____ from you today. After all, you promised to _____. I feel _____. So far, College _____, and today has been _____. I went to a party for the new students _____ - it was _____. I didn't meet _____ (and I don't mean just men, so don't _____!).
   This evening I'm _____ for Judy and David. I'm sure they'll ask me _____. Judy likes going out a lot!
   _____ for now. I'll write again soon, but _____: I'm longing _____ from you!

All my love
Jenny.

③

Jenny has just finished writing to Andrew. The phone rings.

JENNY: 359 0507.

HAROLD: Hullo? Can I speak to Jenny Anderson?

JENNY: Speaking. Who is it?

HAROLD: Harold Lamb. We met at the college party. You gave me your phone
          number. Remember?

JENNY: Well, I didn't exactly *give* it to you . . .

HAROLD: Oh, all right . . . But look, how about coming out for a drink?

JENNY: What, tonight?

HAROLD: Yes. I've got a car. I can come and pick you up.

JENNY: No, it's impossible. I'm sorry, but I'm baby-sitting for my sister.

HAROLD: Oh, what a nuisance. Well, some other time, then. Anyway, I'll see
          you in college.

JENNY: Yes, all right. Thanks for ringing. Bye . . .

④

Jenny decides to answer her mother's letter.

Flat B,

_____

_____

14th, September.

Dear Mum,
Thanks very much for your letter. It was
lovely to hear from you.
Glad to hear you're enjoying the job at
the hospital. Of course, it means you won't
be able to go on any more trips with Dad!

> *Now continue Jenny's letter. Refer to:*
> − something else her mother mentioned in her letter;
> − how she feels about college;
> − the time she spends travelling each day;
> − life in the flat with Judy;
> + one other idea of your own.

Well, I think I'd better stop & do some
work now. I hope my next letter will be a
bit more cheerful!
Love to Dad and Steve. Look after
yourself.
                    Lots of love,
                         Jen.

2. September-October

(1)

Donald and Patsy Anderson are sitting having supper.

PATSY: Have you fixed the dates for your trip yet, darling?

DONALD: More or less. The last week in October and the first ten days in November.

PATSY: And you're both going to Paris – you and John Stone?

DONALD: Yes. And then John'll go on to Holland and Germany and I'll do Italy and Spain.

PATSY: Oh, that'll be nice. You'll be able to see Louise when you're in Italy.

DONALD: Yes, I was planning to go down to Bologna from Milan . . . at least for a couple of days or so.

PATSY: And what exactly are you hoping to find out on this trip?

DONALD: Well, we want to see as many different kinds of hotels as possible. It will help us to see what sort of accommodation tourists expect when they come to Britain. Especially to places like Edinburgh. I mean, do they want to stay in simple hotels – which won't cost so much? Or should we provide more luxury accommodation – which will be more expensive, naturally?

PATSY: Mm, I see what you mean. But surely, different nationalities have different ideas. I mean, look at my American friends – they complain even when they can't get ice in a drink!

DONALD: Yes, that's why we want to do a survey of as many *different* nationalities as possible. And then, perhaps, we can work out a better hotel policy for the future . . .

(2a)

The following morning, Donald Anderson asks his secretary, Sheila Sinclair, to make some arrangements for his trip to Paris.

. . . And then I'd like you to send a letter to the Tourist Board man in Paris. What's his name? Oh, yes, M. Bouvier . . . Lucien Bouvier. At the French Ministry of Tourism. Tell him John and I want to find out what sort of hotels French tourists like . . . You'd better explain exactly what I'm doing – you know, tell him I'm trying to develop a clear policy for our hotels in Edinburgh, so I'm trying to find out what various kinds of people want from an hotel . . . Suggest we spend a day with him in his office – ask him to give me a definite date during the first week in November. And say we'd like to visit several different types of hotel in Paris – we'd be very grateful if he could give us a list of suitable ones to look at. Perhaps he could make the arrangements with the hotel owners, too. I think we should spend about two or three days doing that . . .

6

Use appropriate information from 2a to complete the letter which is sent to M. Bouvier.

Scottish Tourist Board
Argyll Crescent
Edinburgh EG4 2DD

Tel: 031 550 7799
Cables: SCOTOUR

M. Lucien Bouvier,
Ministère de Tourisme,
Rue St. Jacques 95,
PARIS 75006

30 September 19--   Ref:FR/223/1

Dear M. Bouvier,

   I am writing to inform you that John Stone and I are
planning a tour of several European cities during the
late autumn. We shall be in Paris from November 3rd to
the 7th.

   The main reason for our tour is to ..... and to find
out ..... . I have been put in charge of developing a
hotel policy for Edinburgh, so I am ..... .

   We should very much like to ..... in order to take
advantage of your great experience of tourism in France.
Could you tell us ..... .

   There is one other way in which you could help us.
We want to spend two or three days visiting ..... .
I wonder, therefore, if you could ...? I should
also be extremely grateful if you ..... .

   I hope this will not cause you too much trouble. I
look forward very much to meeting you at the beginning
of November.

Yours sincerely,

Donald Anderson,
Research and Development Officer

DA/ss

Now complete M Bouvier's reply to Donald Anderson's letter. Use the information from 2a and 2b to help you.

Ministère De Tourisme
Rue Saint Jacques 95   Paris 75006

Donald Anderson,
Research and Development Officer,
Scottish Tourist Board,
Argyll Crescent,
Edinburgh EG4 2DD,
Scotland.
                                    5 October 19--

Dear ..... ,

     I should certainly like to ..... . The best dates
for me ..... either ..... or ..... . Perhaps you would
let me know which ..... .

     I can certainly introduce you to ..... . I will
discuss your ..... and then send you ..... . I suggest
that you then write to each one directly.

     Please let me know if I ..... . I look forward to
..... .

                         Yours ..... ,

                         Lucien Bouvier,
                         Ministère de Tourisme.

7

Donald Anderson dictates other letters to Sheila Sinclair.

SHEILA: Is that the lot, then, Mr Anderson?

DONALD: Mm, I was just thinking, Sheila. Maybe it would be a good idea to start booking accommodation for the trip. Let's see . . . first, there's Paris . . .

SHEILA: How about the Metropole – where you stayed last time?

DONALD: Yes, that'd be fine.

SHEILA: Two single rooms for you and Mr Stone, then. With bath. November 3rd to the 7th.

DONALD: Mm, yes. Five nights.

SHEILA: And what about Milan?

DONALD: Well, I'll fly there on November 8th, I think.

SHEILA: That's a Saturday, Mr Anderson.

DONALD: Mm. In that case, I'll go straight down to Bologna and stay with my sister. Then I'll come back to Milan on the Tuesday . . .

SHEILA: . . . November 11th . . .

DONALD: Yes. So I'll need a room from the 11th to the 15th. Try the Hotel Imperial in Via Cavour.

SHEILA: Last time, you said it was rather noisy.

DONALD: Yes, I remember. But it's a nice place. Oh, just tell them to make sure it's a quiet room . . .

Write to the Hotel Metropole in Paris to make the reservations. Use the information from 3a to help you.

```
Scottish Tourist Board            Tel: 031  550 7799
       Argyll  Crescent           Cables: SCOTOUR
       Edinburgh EG4 2DD

The Manager,
Hotel Metropole,
Rue St. Jacques 36,
PARIS 75006.

30 September 19--                 Ref:FR/224/1

Dear Sir,

   I should like to reserve two single rooms for .....
```

Mention:
- the names of the people;
- the dates of arrival and departure;
- the type of rooms required.

```
   I should be grateful if you would confirm this booking
as soon as possible.

Yours faithfully,

       Sheila Sinclair
```

Write to the Hotel Imperial, Via Cavour 5, Milan, reserving accommodation for Mr D. Anderson. Use suitable information from the conversation in 3a.

4a

The following day, the phone in Donald Anderson's office rings.

SHEILA: Mr Stone from London is on the line, Mr Anderson.

DONALD: Oh good. Put him through, will you. Hullo John, how are you?

JOHN: Fine, thanks. Well . . . busy, of course! But look, the reason I rang, Don, I wanted to ask you a favour. Do you mind if *I* go to Italy and Spain this time? You see, I'd like to get to know the Tourist Board people there – I've never met any of them personally. That would leave Germany and Holland for you. What do you feel about that?

DONALD: Yes . . . well . . . yes . . ., that makes sense, I suppose . . .

JOHN: You don't sound too sure, Don.

DONALD: Well, it's just that I was hoping to see my sister Louise in Bologna. Doesn't matter, though. You go to Italy this time. Patsy and I are probably going there in the spring, anyway.

JOHN: Thanks, Don.

DONALD: Now, I've already asked my secretary to book me a room in Milan from November 11th to the 15th.

JOHN: Oh, I've got friends in Milan. I'll stay with them.

DONALD: Well, in that case, I'll get Sheila to cancel the reservation. Of course, you should go to Bologna as well as Milan, and Venice and Rome.

JOHN: Any suggestions for a hotel in Bologna?

DONALD: Well, I always stay with my sister. She could put you up, I'm sure.

JOHN: Oh . . . I think I ought to stay in an hotel.

DONALD: All right, though you should meet Louise and her husband. Tell you what, I've got to write to her anyway, to tell her I'm not coming. I'll ask her to book you a room.

JOHN: Would you? That'll be a great help. I'll go to Milan first and then go on to Bologna . . . let's say November 13th to the 15th . . .

4b

Refer to the letter you wrote in 3c, and write to the Hotel Imperial in Milan again, cancelling Donald Anderson's reservation. Set your letter out like a business letter (see 2b) and begin:

Dear Sir,
With reference to my letter of 30 September in which I reserved . . .

Now continue.

4c

Write a short letter from John Stone to his friends in Milan (make up suitable names for them). Say that you are coming to Milan from November 8th to 13th, and ask them to put you up.

(5a)

That evening, when Donald gets home from the office, feeling rather tired, he finds the following note.

> Darling —
> Gone to concert at S's school.
> Sorry I forgot to tell you about
> it! Back about 9. Supper
> in fridge.
>   Love —P.
> P.S. Judy phoned. David has a
> small TV job. And Jenny's
> passed her first typing test!

(5b)

Donald feels rather cross. He wanted to spend the evening with his wife – and he does not like cold suppers! After he has finished his supper, he decides to write to his sister Louise in Bologna. Complete his letter.

> ### 18 Craigmillar Road, Edinburgh EG6 7YY
> ### Tel: 031 556 1342
>
>   30th September
>
> Dear Louise,
>
> How are you both? We're all quite well, although I'm sitting on my own at the moment, feeling sorry for myself and writing letters! *(Give reason. Include news of Jenny and Judy.)*
>
> I'm afraid that I shan't be able to come and see you in November after all. *(Explain why.)* However, a colleague of mine, John Stone, will be coming instead. *(Give reason.)* Do you think you could possibly book a hotel room for him? *(Mention dates, and suggest she takes him out for a meal.)*
>
> As I said in my last letter, Patsy and I are going to spend two weeks in Dubrovnik in May. We shall be driving down to Ancona, so...*(Ask if you can stay a couple of days with her on the way.)*
>
> Give my love to Piero. Sorry about November - but hope to see you in May!
>
>   Much love,
>
>   Donald

When Patsy and Steve get back from the concert, Donald is in a really bad mood.

PATSY: Sorry we're back so late, darling. The concert was a terrific success, though. It's a pity you missed it . . .

DONALD: Well, nobody told me anything about it, did they . . . Oh, Stephen, I'd like to have a word with you.

PATSY: Donald!
(She goes out.)

DONALD: Now look here. You're spending far too much time with this pop group of yours. You seem to do nothing else. What about your school work?

STEVE: Oh, Dad, it's all right. Anyway, this is the first concert we've had this term.

DONALD: And what about all the evenings you've spent rehearsing for it? Anyway, why didn't you tell me it was tonight?

STEVE: Well . . . I meant to . . . but . . .

DONALD: Hm! I suppose you thought I'd stop you. Look, Stephen, I don't like finding things out at the last minute. And especially from someone else.

STEVE: Well, I really did forget, Dad. There's been so much to do, with all the rehearsals and arrangements. *And* school work. Oh, don't worry, I haven't neglected that!

DONALD: Maybe not. But you wander around the house looking half asleep most of the time. Dead white face and great shadows under your eyes. You're obviously not getting enough sleep – or fresh air.

STEVE: Oh Dad – it's my life! I'm old enough to . . .

DONALD: Hm. Well, just you make sure you're in bed by eleven every night during the week. The weekend's a different matter.

STEVE: Oh hell!!!
(Steve goes out, banging the door.)

Stephen goes up to his room – but not to bed. He is absolutely furious! Write the letter he sends to his Dutch penfriend, Harm Reinders. Refer to the pop concert and the argument with his father.

Write Harm's reply.

3. September-November

(1)

John Stone and his wife are finishing supper one evening.

DIANA: This coffee really is revolting! It costs enough, too. When I think of that heavenly stuff we had in Italy . . .

JOHN: Well, I'll bring some back with me. I'll be there next month.

DIANA: What – Italy? You're going to Italy? You didn't tell me.

JOHN: It's only just been decided. I'm going there instead of Donald Anderson. Strictly on business, of course.

DIANA: Business! Huh! Visiting all the nicest places in Europe, eating huge meals and pretending you're working. And lots of pretty women to entertain you.

JOHN: Don't be silly, Di.

DIANA: Well, why is it *I* never go with you? Other wives go, but never me. There must be some reason.

JOHN: Look, you know very well it's because of the children. Anyway, isn't the new au pair girl arriving soon?

DIANA: Oh – Anne-Marie? Yes, but I don't know exactly when she's coming. She's very vague.

JOHN: Well, why don't you write and tell her you must have a definite date. Or, better, send a telegram. Then she'll realise it's urgent. You can join me in Italy in the middle of November. She'll be used to the children by then . . .

(2a)

Next morning, Diana Stone sends this telegram to Anne-Marie Mignen.

Post Office International Telegram

TO	MIGNEN. 14 RUE LOUISE. NANTES.

PLEASE SEND DATE TIME PLACE OF ARRIVAL STOP   NEED YOU URGENTLY OCTOBER TENTH STOP   REPLY IMMEDIATELY STOP   STONE

Name and Address of Sender (Not to be Telegraphed)
DIANA STONE   26 CHESTNUT DRIVE
OXTED   SURREY .... Telephone No. ....

2b

Complete this letter from Anne-Marie. She wrote it before she got the telegram from Mrs Stone.

```
                                              Nantes
                                              28 September 19--

Dear Mrs Stone,

        I am writing to tell you that I am coming to England on October
10th.  I have decided to come by ..... because it is ..... .  My .....
gets into ..... at ..... .
        ..... , so it is not necessary to meet me, but I will telephone
you when I arrive.


                                      Yours sincerely,

                                      Anne-Marie Mignen.
```

3a

Anne-Marie has arrived, and Mrs Stone is telling her about her duties.

MRS STONE: ... Of course, I'd like you to help me a bit in the house, Anne-Marie. And do the shopping. That'll be good practice for your English.

ANNE-MARIE: Yes, of course, Mrs Stone. Oh, I see my room is next to Mark's. Does he wake up much at night?

MRS STONE: No, hardly ever. The children are no trouble, in fact ...

ANNE-MARIE: Jane and Simon seem to quarrel a lot.

MRS STONE: Oh, that was just today. They're very well-behaved as a rule.

ANNE-MARIE: And all the children go to school?

MRS STONE: Yes, I take them myself in the car and pick them up in the afternoon. But I would like you to fetch them some afternoons. You see, I have lots of meetings. I belong to the Conservative Women's Association ...

ANNE-MARIE: And what about my language lessons?

MRS STONE: Oh, you'll have plenty of time to study.

ANNE-MARIE: Yes, but I want to go to a language school.

MRS STONE: Well, perhaps we can find someone here in Oxted to help you. Many of my friends have lived abroad and most of them speak some French, you know!

ANNE-MARIE: Yes, but that's not the point, Mrs Stone. I need *proper* lessons.

MRS STONE: Well, just leave that to me. I'm sure we can find the right person for you. And of course, I'll help too. I've always wanted to teach ...

ANNE-MARIE: Hm!

This is the letter which Anne-Marie sends to an English friend in Cambridge.

26 Chestnut Drive,
Oxted, Surrey.
October 14th.

Dear Anna,
I've been here four days now and I thought I'd write and tell you about it.
It's nice to be back in England, but one thing is quite certain: I don't like this family. I don't like Oxted very much, either.

Now continue, referring to Anne-Marie's problems:
Mrs Stone difficult woman/makes me work very hard/big house/
three young children/badly behaved and argue a lot/no proper
language lessons

However, I hope things will get better, otherwise I don't think I can stay here six months. Can we meet one day in London? — I'm free on Tuesdays.

Love,
Anne-Marie

4a

One evening towards the end of October, Diana Stone comes into the kitchen while Anne-Marie is washing the supper dishes.

MRS STONE: That was a nice supper you cooked, Anne-Marie. You must tell me how you made that sauce.

ANNE-MARIE: Oh, did you like it, Mrs Stone? I'm glad.

MRS STONE: Yes, it's the best thing you've cooked so far. In fact, your cooking has improved a lot. So has your English.

ANNE-MARIE: Yes, but I'm not *really* making any progress. I told you – I need proper lessons.

MRS STONE: Well, we can do something about that when I come back from Italy.

ANNE-MARIE: Italy? You're going to Italy?

MRS STONE: Yes, John's going there on a business trip and I'm going to join him for a few days.

ANNE-MARIE: And you're taking the children too?

MRS STONE: Goodness, no. They mustn't miss school. Besides, they'll be quite safe and happy with you, Anne-Marie.

ANNE-MARIE: But, Mrs Stone, I can't stay here alone with three children. It's too much . . .

MRS STONE: Of course you can. You'll be perfectly all right.

ANNE-MARIE: But the agency – they told me I would only *help* you.

MRS STONE: Well, this *is* helping me. Now, let's not discuss it any more. I shall leave on the 8th of November for about ten days . . .

4b

Complete this letter which Anne-Marie writes to her friend Anna in Cambridge. Read Anna's reply in 4c first.

> Oxted
> 25th October
>
> Dear Anna,
> I feel absolutely desperate!
> Mrs Stone _____. Of course, I've refused.
> Can I _____? I won't be any trouble.
> Of course, it would be nice to find a
> job in Cambridge. _____? If I can't,
> _____
> Please write soon and let me know
> if _____.
>
> Love,
> Anne-Marie.

As soon as Anna gets Anne-Marie's letter, she writes back.

42 Saint John's Road, Cambridge.

27 October.

Dear Anne-Marie,

I've just got your letter. You're absolutely right. Of course you can't stay with that family. Mrs Stone sounds awful.

Yes, you can come and stay with us. And, what's more, there's even the possibility of a job. You see, the woman who lives next door runs a students' house for the university, & she needs someone to help her. It would mean doing a bit of everything — cooking, cleaning etc., but she's very nice and I'm sure you'd like it. Especially with all the male students — there's a shortage of women in Cambridge, you know!

Come as soon as you like. See you soon.

Love,
Anna.

P.S. There are some good language schools in Cambridge and plenty of social life!

Write a note from Anne-Marie to Anna saying when she is coming to Cambridge.

This is the letter Anne-Marie sends to Mrs Stone from Cambridge.

> 42 Saint John's Road,
> Cambridge.
> 9th November.

Dear Mrs Stone,

When I left your house, I forgot my raincoat. It's hanging in the cupboard in the hall with the other coats. Would you please send it to me?

I'm enjoying life in Cambridge. I've made lots of friends here and I've found a good language school.

I'm sorry you couldn't go to Italy, but I'm sure the children are happy that you are at home. I hope you are not still angry with me.

> Yours sincerely,
> Anne-Marie Mignen.

Write Mrs Stone's reply.

4. October

Judy is speaking on the phone to a friend of her sister's.

. . . No, I've no idea what time she'll be home . . . yes, all right, I'll take a message. Just let me get a bit of paper and a pen. Now, what did you say your name was? . . . Hang on a minute, let me get that down first . . . Harold Lamb . . . OK . . . Where do you want her to meet you? . . . The Camden Head pub. What time? . . . About 7.30. All right. But if she's not back before then? . . . Oh, so you'll be there until 8.30 . . . Wait a minute. Damn, I've dropped the pen. Sorry – what number did you say she could phone you at? . . . 226 3050 after 8.30. OK. I've got all that. I'm going out myself, but I'll leave her a note. Bye.

Write the note that Judy leaves for Jenny. Mention the important details from the conversation in 1a. Begin:

Harold Lamb rang . . .

A few days later, Judy and Jenny have an argument.

JUDY: *You're* fed up! Just because you have to baby-sit sometimes. Well, I don't think it's very much to ask. David and I don't go out *that* often. Besides, you don't exactly do much in the house.

JENNY: What do you mean?

JUDY: Well, I even have to wash the bath after you've used it! And the other day I had to give your room a proper clean.

JENNY: I didn't ask you to!

JUDY: Well, thanks! And then I spend half my time taking down messages for you. People are always ringing up.

JENNY: Well, I do the same for you.

JUDY: And how! Yesterday, when *Corn Poppy* rang up, you got the message all wrong. Now I've got to write to them and apologise – and I probably won't even get that order. And, in case you didn't realise it, that means MONEY for us . . .

18

2b

That evening, after their argument, Jenny writes to her mother. A few days later, Patsy replies (see 2c). Complete Jenny's letter.

Flat B, 16 Upper Street,
London N.1.

15th. October.

Dear Mum,

I really don't think I can stand living here with Judy and David ....

Now continue (referring to both 2a and 2c). You may make use of these connecting phrases:

For one thing, . . . Besides, . . . On top of that . . . Now if I . . . And then I'd be able to . . .

Please talk it over with Dad and let me know as soon as possible.

Lots of love
Jen.

2c

18 Craigmillar Road, Edinburgh EG6 7YY
Tel: 031 556 1342

18 October

Dear Jenny,

I was quite upset by your letter. I know it can't be easy, living in a small flat with Judy, David and a baby. But there's no alternative, I'm afraid. I've talked it over with your father and we simply cannot afford the extra money.

You say it wouldn't be so expensive if you shared a flat with 3 or 4 other girls. But it would cost <u>at least</u> £25-30 a month + extras. That's quite a lot of money, you know! So I'm afraid the answer is NO.

But I do understand how you feel. As you say, you aren't free to invite your friends home and you have to baby-sit, etc. But that was part of the agreement, wasn't it? After all, we don't pay Judy much rent for the room.

So do try to be a little more patient, will you, darling. After all, it's only for a few months. When you've finished your course, and have a job, you'll be able to do as you please.

Love from us both,

Mum.

19

Complete this letter which Judy sends to Mrs Sheila Waites, the owner of Corn Poppy, 5 Trafalgar Street, Brighton. Use appropriate connectors from those listed below. Set your letter out like a business letter.

```
                          Flat B .....
        Mrs Sheila Waites,
        ..............,
        ..............,
        ..............,                 ..................

        Dear Mrs Waites,
          I am writing to apologise for not sending the three dozen
        rings you ordered.
          ......, my sister did not explain that you wanted the rings
        immediately.  ......, I do have a dozen rings available,
        ........ I could let you have straightaway.  I could ........
        make the other two dozen in about ten days.
          ........, I shall quite understand if you want to cancel the
        order.  ......., I apologise very much for the confusion.
        Yours sincerely,

        Judy Cameron
        Judy Cameron
```

| *however* | *of course* | *unfortunately* |
| *meanwhile* | *then* | *which* |

Write Mrs Waites' reply. You may **confirm** the order, asking for immediate delivery, or **cancel** it, giving your reason(s) (e.g. the customer was a visitor from abroad who has now left the country).

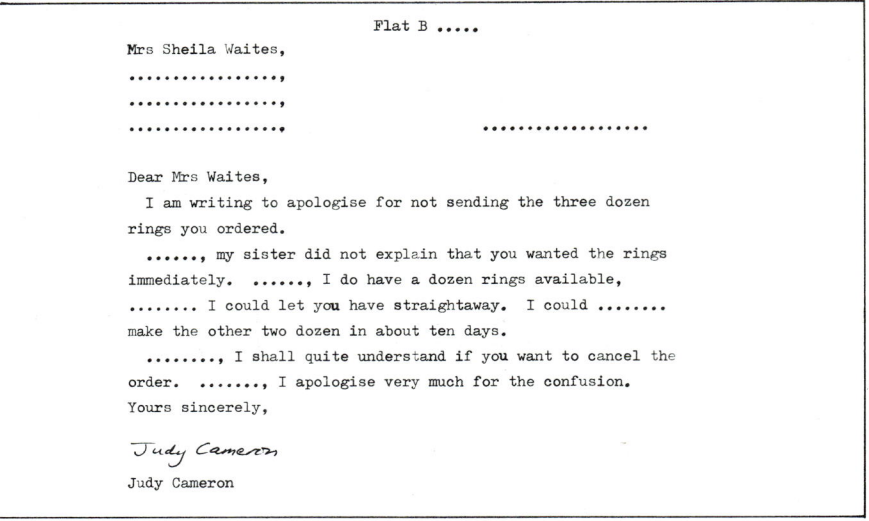

```
TRIAD     17a Holywell Street
          Oxford OR5 7BW

                        ref: 75/18/10        18.x.19--

Dear Ms Cameron,

Thank you for your last consignment of one dozen silver necklaces.
These proved a great success with our customers and we sold them all
within a week.  A cheque for £60 is enclosed.

We think your jewellery would make very attractive Christmas presents,
so we would like to place a further order with you for these items:

            1.     2 doz. silver and topaz rings.
            2.     2 doz. necklaces (like the previous ones).
            3.     1 doz. silver chains with medallions.

However, the consignment must reach us by 20 November at the latest,
since people start shopping early for Christmas.  Could you undertake
to complete the order by that date?

                          Yours sincerely,

                          UgoDeMarco
                          Ugo De Marco,
                          Director

Ms J. Cameron,
16 Upper Street,
LONDON N1.
```

4b

David is writing letters. Judy is very excited and shows him her letter from Triad.

JUDY: Just look at this letter from Triad, David. It's fantastic, isn't it?
DAVID *(reading the letter)*: Terrific!
JUDY: The thing is, though, I can't manage a big order like this all by myself. I've worked it out – it would take at least a couple of months.
DAVID: Mm, that's a pity.
JUDY: Of course, if you could lend a hand . . .
DAVID: You know I'd love to. But what happens if I get a part in that TV series?
JUDY: Well, I've got to say yes or no to them. So it's really up to you . . .

4c

Decide whether or not David helps Judy. Then write her reply to Triad. If he **agrees**, confirm that the order can be delivered by November 20th. If he **does not agree**, offer them a smaller number of items.

4d

Write Triad's reply to Judy's letter.

5. November

John Stone and Donald Anderson are sitting having a drink in Paris after their day with M. Bouvier.

JOHN: Well, they weren't as critical of our hotel accommodation as I expected!

DONALD: Mm, I was surprised, too.

JOHN: If I'm right, the main thing that worries French tourists in Britain is that they don't know exactly how much a room is going to cost them when they take it.

DONALD: Yes, that's a good point. There should be a notice in each room with the price of the room on it . . .

JOHN: . . . and saying exactly what that price includes.

DONALD: Yes, and in general it should be easier to get lists of hotels for each town – as you can over here, at any tourist office.

JOHN: Yes, I made a note of that. It was another good point, I thought.

DONALD: And on the whole, they weren't *so* critical of British food.

JOHN: No. And they were especially keen on the 'Tourist Menu' idea. I think we should recommend that more places adopt it . . .

Complete part of John Stone's report using suitable information from the conversation in 1a.

```
As far as hotel accommodation is concerned, the representatives
of the French Tourist Board ..... .  However, they pointed out
that French tourists ....., and for this reason we recommend
that ..... in each room, which should also state exactly ..... .
In addition, it should be easier to get ....., as in most
European countries.

Similarly, there were no strong criticisms of ....., but all
the representatives ....., and we therefore recommend that
..... .
```

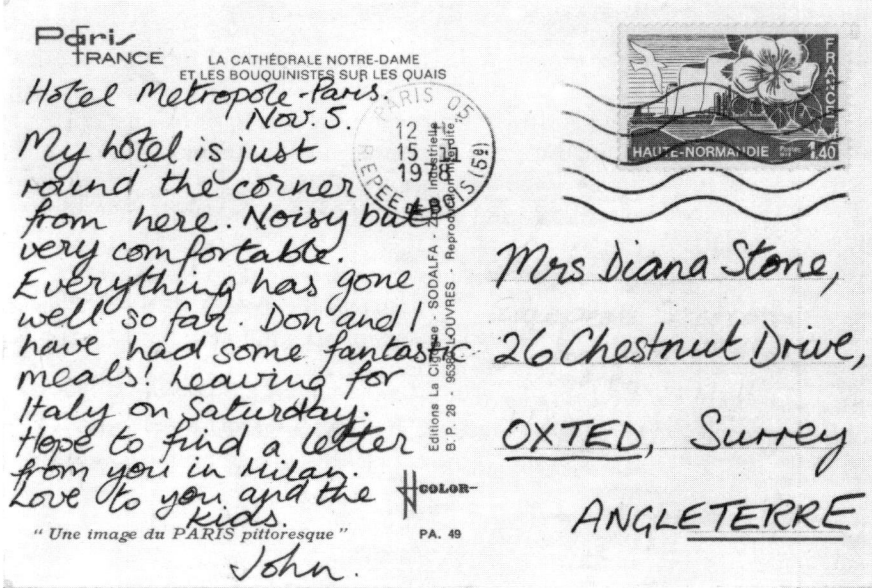

Paris
FRANCE
LA CATHÉDRALE NOTRE-DAME
ET LES BOUQUINISTES SUR LES QUAIS

Hôtel Metropole - Paris.
Nov. 5.
My hotel is just round the corner from here. Noisy but very comfortable. Everything has gone well so far. Don and I have had some fantastic meals! Leaving for Italy on Saturday. Hope to find a letter from you in Milan. Love to you and the kids.

" Une image du PARIS pittoresque "   PA. 49

John.

Mrs Diana Stone,

26 Chestnut Drive,

OXTED, Surrey

ANGLETERRE

2b

Write a postcard from Donald Anderson in Paris to any member(s) of his family.

Donald Anderson is in Amsterdam. Harm Reinders has telephoned him and they arrange to meet.

DONALD: Actually, Harm, I'm very glad you rang. You see, I'm here because I'm trying to find out what tourists want when they come to Britain. That's why I'm visiting several countries.

HARM: What sort of things are you interested in, Mr Anderson?

DONALD: Well, in particular, accommodation and food.

HARM: But I always stay with Steve when I come to England – I mean Scotland!

DONALD: All the same, you know lots of young people here. Students, for example. Now that's an interesting area for us. Do we do enough to provide students with the right sort of accommodation in Britain? And can they get meals at the right prices?

HARM: Well, of course I'll talk to my friends. And then what?

DONALD: Well, let's see. I'm leaving for Germany the day after tomorrow. That won't give you much time. Could you write to me in Edinburgh, giving me your ideas?

HARM: Yes, of course I'll do that, Mr Anderson . . .

Write the letter which Harm sends to Donald Anderson in Edinburgh, referring to the following points:
- whether students mind sharing rooms with people they do not know;
- whether they would like more hostel accommodation and/or camping sites;
- whether they prefer to be in the centre of cities or outside;
- whether they want accommodation with or without meals;
- what kind of meals they like;
- whether they would like to stay with local families;
- . . .

You may wish to use the following:

but generally   *on the whole*
it's always better   *some people . . ., while others . . .*
of course   *you have to remember*
on the other hand

Donald Anderson writes this letter from Amsterdam to his wife.

Hotel Centraal
Leidesplein
Amsterdam

11 November

Darling,

I was hoping to find a letter from you here; I suppose it will arrive after I've left!

Continue the letter. Refer to:
- the success of the trip so far;
- the meeting with Harm;
- your impressions of Amsterdam.

Inquire about:
- Steve's behaviour;
- Patsy's work;
- the rest of the family.

Well, that's about all for now. I hope to hear from you in Munich. If not, I shall phone.

All my love,

This is the letter which John Stone finds waiting for him in Milan.

> 26 Chestnut Drive,
> Oxted, Surrey
>
> Tel: Oxted 3971
>
> 6th November.
>
> Dearest John,
>
> Why haven't you written or rung me from Paris as you promised? I know you have a pretty full programme, but at least you could find time in the evenings. I suppose you're out every night.
>
> Life here has been rather dismal. The weather has been rotten. First Simon got a cold, then Mark — and now I think I'm going to catch it. I feel really depressed. I hate being here on my own. And just think —— I could have gone to Italy ...
>
> One good bit of news: They've made me Secretary of the Conservative Women's Association. Of course, it will take up a lot of time — but aren't you proud of me?
>
> By the way, the car has broken down. It's a bore, but I think I'll leave it till you get back. I can manage without it.
>
> I think I'll go to bed early — it will help my cold. The children all send their love. A note from Simon is enclosed. Be good now, and don't flirt with those Italian girls!
>
> All my love,
>
> Di.
>
> P.S. The electricity bill has just come in. It's enormous.

Write the short note from Simon to his father which Diana Stone encloses in her letter. You can refer to:

- your cold;
- what you are doing at school;
- any other ideas of your own.

Ask for a present from Italy.

26

5a

These are some notes which John Stone made while he was in Bologna.

Louise and Piero took me to their favourite restaurant here: the Torre Eiffel. It's a very simple place: the husband does the cooking and the wife (who's French) waits at table. I had a fantastic onion soup (<u>her</u> recipe, which she gave me!) and something called 'bollito' (several different kinds of boiled meat with a green sauce). I'm going to have dinner with Louise and Piero this evening - she's promised to make me 'tortellini' (one of the specialities of Bologna).

After dinner, we walked around the city and then spent some time sitting on the steps of the Cathedral in the main square. Even at 11 o'clock at night, it was full of people talking and arguing. It was a marvellous experience - just like a Fellini film! I suppose the wine helped!!!

 5b

Write the letter John Stone sends to his wife from Bologna. Refer to certain points in Diana's letter (4a) and also make use of some of the information in 5a.

6. November-December

Patsy keeps a diary. This is what she writes while Donald is away.

November

Tuesday
318–47   Week 46
○ Full Moon

14

Letter from Don (in A'dam) this morning. Trip has been a great success so far. Looks as if the letter I wrote to A'dam has got lost — or arrived after he left. Must send an express one to Munich today. Steve's been behaving very well. Has stayed in most evenings this week working (at least he's been up in his room all the time!) Just hope he keeps it up. Must tell D. because I know he worries a lot about S. (too much, I think). Good news from London. Judy says Jen seems to be settling down — at least she doesn't grumble quite so much. Also has a boy-friend (Judy doesn't like him!) Hope it isn't serious, because Andrew's such a nice boy (better not say anything about this to D.) It looks as if David may get a regular job at last — something to do with TV. What a relief! Job at the hospital is great fun — tiring sometimes, but I feel I'm seeing LIFE! Only this morning

December
M T W T F S S | M T W T F S S | M T W T F S S | M T W T F S S | M T W T F S S | M T
          1 2 3 | 4 5 6 7 8 9 10 | 11 12 13 14 15 16 17 | 18 19 20 21 22 23 24 | 25 26 27 28 29 30 31 |

Either **invent** any suitable incident (funny or serious) to continue the entry in Patsy's diary about what happened at the hospital that morning, or **describe** the story shown in the picture sequence below.

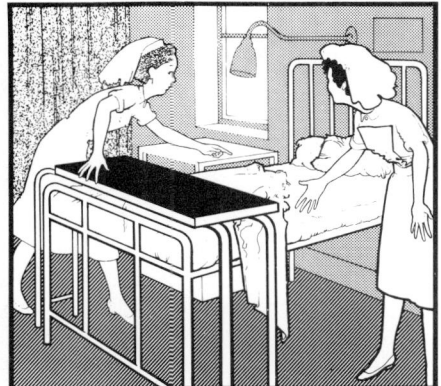

Write the express letter Patsy sends to Donald in Munich. Refer to his letter in Unit 5 3c, and make use of the information in Patsy's diary entry.

2a

Patsy has been talking to a friend about her work in the hospital.

JEAN: . . . Well, I must say, Patsy, you make hospital life sound quite fascinating! You should write a novel about it!

PATSY: Actually, I have just finished writing a short story.

JEAN: What are you going to do with it? Publish it?

PATSY: Oh, I hadn't really thought about it. I just wrote it to pass the time while Don's away.

JEAN: Well, if I were you, I'd send it to a magazine. You know, a friend of mine got £25 for a story she wrote.

PATSY: You really think I should try to get it published?

JEAN: Well, you've got nothing to lose, have you? Why don't you try *Women's Life* – or *People and Places*, perhaps. They both go in for stories of the human interest kind.

2b

This is the covering letter which Patsy sends with her story to both magazines.

---

18 Craigmillar Road, Edinburgh EG6 7YY
Tel: 031 556 1342

                                                    16 November 19--

Dear Editor,

    I enclose a story I have written, which I have called
Backwards and Forwards.

Now continue. Expand these phrases:
story about 5000 words long/about life in a hospital/based on personal
observation/am a ward receptionist in our local hospital/keep a daily
diary/ all the events true

    I hope you will find the story suitable for publication.

                                    Yours faithfully,

                                    Patsy Anderson
                                    Patsy Anderson.

These are the replies which Patsy gets from both magazines.

Women's Life
127 The Strand
London WCIB 7HA
01 734 5252

ref: AG/9   30 November 19—

Miss Patsy Anderson,
18 Craigmillar Road,
Edinburgh EG6 7YY.

Dear Miss Anderson,

Thank you for letting us see your story 'Backwards and Forwards'.

Although I liked your story, I regret that we cannot publish it in its present form for the following reasons:

1 Our maximum story length is 3500 words. Your story at present runs to approximately 5000 words, which is far too long.

2 Our readers prefer stories with a romantic element. This is completely missing from your story.

Then, I also felt that the personality of the narrator did not come across very clearly — but this, perhaps, is a minor detail.

If you would like to try rewriting your story to meet these requirements, we should be glad to reconsider it for publication.

Yours sincerely,

Sheila Reddaway

Sheila Reddaway (Miss)
Story Editor

⊕m/SR

and People Places
178 Greengate   Manchester 20H 6B
Tel: 061 834 9898

December 2 19—   Ref: 79/2/A

Dear Ms Anderson,

Thank you for sending us your story of hospital life entitled Backwards and Forwards.

I enjoyed reading it immensely and I especially liked the lively, natural style with which you described events.

I am therefore writing to say that we shall be pleased to publish your story (probably in early January). Our standard fee for stories of this length is £30, and I trust this is acceptable. A cheque for this amount will be sent to you upon publication.

May I ask whether you have — or would be willing to write — other stories about hospital life of a similar kind? We feel that our readers would enjoy a series of, let us say, five such stories.

I look forward to hearing from you in the near future.

Yours very sincerely,

Arnold Jackson

Arnold Jackson   rf/AJ
Editor

Ms Patsy Anderson,
18 Craigmillar Road,
Edinburgh EG6 7YY,
Scotland

(3b)

Patsy replies to both editors on the same day. Write the letters which she sends to each of them.

31

7. January

Judy is talking to David about a letter she has had from Steve.

DAVID: What's Steve got to say for himself, then?

JUDY: Well, he's terribly excited about that pop group of his. Seems they're making quite a name for themselves in Edinburgh.

DAVID: Oh, good for Steve.

JUDY: And he wants to take the group abroad this summer. Probably to Amsterdam. He's got a friend there – Harm. You remember him?

DAVID: Mm.

JUDY: Something I don't understand, though.

DAVID: What's that?

JUDY: Well, he says Mum's had a story published. Doesn't say what it's about, though, or where. It's odd she's never mentioned it to me. I think I'll write and ask her what it's all about. We aren't going out this evening, are we?

DAVID: How can we? I simply must get these letters off tonight. Otherwise I'll *never* get a job.

JUDY: In that case, then, I'll answer Steve's letter and write to Mum as well.

This is the letter which Judy got from Steve (see 1a).

Edinburgh.Jan.4.

Dear Judy,

Thanks a lot for the silver ring you + DAvid sent me for Christmas. I think all the other members of the group (damn! I can't type!) would like one too!

Continue Steve's letter. Refer to:
- the success of the pop group in Edinburgh;
- your plans to go abroad, possibly to Amsterdam;
- Mum's story;
  + any other news.

Glad your work is going well and look forward to seeing David on TV oneof these days!

love

S.

Write Judy's reply to Steve's letter. You may say:

- you are glad about the success of his group;
- you are pleased he liked the Christmas present (If the rest of the group want rings, you will be pleased to take an order!);
- you did not know that Mum had written a story;
- David is still trying to get a job in the theatre;
    + any other news.

Write Judy's letter to her mother.

You *must*:
- mention you have had a letter from Steve, who has referred to her story;
- ask for more information about it.

You *may*:
- refer to David, saying that he is still trying to get a job;
- say how pleased you are about Steve's group;
- ask after Dad.

Write Patsy's reply to Judy's letter. Refer to Unit 6 (especially 3a and 3b).

David gets the following phone call from his agent, Marcia Lang.

David . . . Marcia here . . . Look, I've just heard from Manchester. They're doing a production of *Romeo and Juliet* in February and they want someone to play Mercutio . . . has to be able to dance and sing . . . and look good in Elizabethan costume . . . Who's the director? Frank Giles — he's done some excellent work up there. Yes, I think you stand a good chance of getting it. How long is it for? . . . Well, three weeks' rehearsal on half-salary, and then three weeks' performance . . . and I reckon there's a good chance of staying on if they like you. Look, write to Frank and say I'm your agent, and ask for an audition. Send him one of our agency forms . . .

David writes to ask for an audition.

16 Upper Street, London N.1.

4 January 19—

Frank Giles,
Everyman Theatre,
Brick Lane,
Manchester M20 2BZ.

Dear Mr Giles,
 My agent, Marcia Lang, has told me that you are looking
for someone to play the part of Mercutio in your production
of <u>Romeo and Juliet.</u>

Continue David's letter:
 — mention that you can dance and sing;
 — say that you are enclosing photographs of yourself in Elizabethan
  costume;
 — say that you would like an audition;
 — ask when and where the auditions will be held;
 — give your phone number.

 Looking forward to hearing from you,
Yours sincerely,

David Cameron
David Cameron.

David writes to Robert Woods, a friend of his, who is acting with a company in Exeter.

16, Upper St. N.1.

15 Jan

Dear Bob,

It was good to hear from you after so long. I'm delighted you like it so much down at Exeter & that everything is going well. Lucky you!

I wish I had some cheerful news for you, but frankly, things aren't going well. Do you know, I've written over 20 letters asking for jobs in the last 2 weeks, and so far No oNE has shown the slightest interest in my talents!

I did get an audition for Mercutio in the Manchester production of R & J — but didn't get the part. Sometimes I wonder if I'll _ever_ get a job.

And between you and me, Judy is getting pretty fed up. She manages to make enough to keep us with her jewellery, and I've been helping too — but there's no future in it for me, obviously.

If you have a chance, put in a word for me with the people at Exeter, will you? I'd be very grateful.

All the best.

yours,
David.

P.S. I'm sending my 'vital statistics' just in case!

This is the reference form which the agency sends to theatre directors when David is applying for a job. Complete it and invent facts you do not know.

```
ACTOR'S NAME ...................................................

ADDRESS .......................................................

TEL.NO: ....................... DATE OF BIRTH .............

HEIGHT ........................ WEIGHT ....................

COLOUR OF HAIR ............... COLOUR OF EYES ............

ANY DISTINGUISHING FEATURES ...............................

WHERE WAS HE TRAINED? .....................................

FROM ........................ TO .......................

PARTS PLAYED DURING LAST TERM AT DRAMA SCHOOL .............

...............................................................

...............................................................

CAN HE SING? ................ DANCE? ....................

PLAY ANY MUSICAL INSTRUMENTS? .............................

FOREIGN LANGUAGES SPOKEN ..................................

DETAILS OF PROFESSIONAL WORK
RADIO .......................................................

...............................................................

TELEVISION ..................................................

...............................................................

THEATRE (SAY WHERE) .........................................

...............................................................

OTHER WORK (COMMERCIALS, MODELLING, ETC.) .................

...............................................................

IS HE MARRIED? ................ CHILDREN? .................

ANY OTHER DETAILS ...........................................

...............................................................
```

THE MORLEY THEATRE EXETER

Telephone: (0392) 5492

David Cameron,
16 Upper Street,
London   N1.

January 22nd, 19—

Dear Mr Cameron,

Your friend Robert Woods has mentioned your name to me and has also shown me your photographs and agent's form.

As it happens, we are planning to put on a special Shaw season, which will open on 2 March and will run for six weeks. For this we shall need at least one other actor. We wonder whether you would be free for this period?

How soon could you come down for an audition? If this is satisfactory, we should be pleased to offer you an eight week contract (two weeks of rehearsal before the season opens). I think we could promise you at least one major role.

I look forward to hearing from you as soon as possible.

Yours sincerely,

Toby Rogers.

Toby Rogers,
Artistic Director

David discusses this offer with Judy. It means he will have to go out of London for two months, leaving her behind. Decide what their decision is and write David's reply to Toby Rogers' letter.

If David decides to go to Exeter, write his letter to Bob Woods thanking him for his help and inquiring about accommodation for the period.

If David decides not to go to Exeter, write his letter to Bob Woods giving the reasons. for his decision.

Write Bob Woods' reply to David's letter (either 4c or 4d).

8. February

Jenny is talking to Ros, a friend of hers at the secretarial college.

JENNY: What sort of things do they ask you to do in this exam, then?

ROS: Well, it's never exactly the same twice running. But basically it's a sort of psychological test.

JENNY: Meaning?

ROS: They're trying to find out your strengths and weaknesses.

JENNY: How?

ROS: Well, for instance, they give you a pile of letters to answer. Then, as soon as you settle down, the phone starts ringing – people keep coming in and interrupting you. Sometimes they even try to make you lose your temper!

JENNY: Sounds terrifying!

ROS: Oh, it's not so bad. The main thing is, just keep cool. And make sure you answer all the letters.

JENNY: I'm sure I'll fail!

During her exam, Jenny is asked to play the part of someone who has just begun work as a hotel receptionist. This is one of the letters she has to answer.

Northern
Radar
Research
Unit   Craigie House, GLASGOW 8PR 2FA

Telephone 041 552 4361   Cables NORA Telex 23356 NORA RU

Ref: XGH/365   3 February 19--

Dear Sir,

   Please refer to our letter of 14 January
(ref: XGH/364), in which we reserved accommodation
(5 single rooms) for the delegates attending the
National Telecommunications Conference from 9 - 15
February.

   We very much regret that we are obliged to cancel
this reservation, since our delegates will be unable
to attend the Conference, and we should be obliged if
you would return our deposit of £25.

   Please accept our apologies for this late
cancellation.

Yours ever,

Mary Hines

pp Richard F. Wallace,
Director, NRRU

*Miss Anderson: please inform
them that there is a
cancellation charge of
£2 per person, unless
7 days' clear notice
is given.
   Send a cheque for the
balance.   RP*

The Manager,
Pelham Hotel,
Pelham Crescent,
London SW7A 8HJ   cfs/MH

38

2b

Write Jenny's reply to the letter in 2a, taking into account the instructions written on that letter.

PELHAM HOTEL

Pelham Crescent
London SW7A 8HJ

01 828 7197   cables : PELHO

Ref: 2/3/5   5th February 19--

Dear Ms Haines,

    This is with reference to your letter of ..... , informing us .....

    I regret to inform you that ..... because ..... . A cheque for .....

                      Yours sincerely,

                      Jenny Anderson.

2c

This is another letter which Jenny has to answer during her exam.

                                 Meadowcroft, Radyr, Glamorgan, South Wales.

The Manager,
Pelham Hotel,
Pelham Crescent,
LONDON SW7.   2nd February 19--

Dear Sir,

    I should like to reserve the following accommodation for the period 20th.-25th. February:

              1 double room (with <u>bath</u>)
              1 single room (without bath)

    Would you please confirm that this accommodation is available, and also tell me the cost per room.

                      Yours faithfully,

                      Bryn Owen
                    Bryn Owen

Handwritten note in margin:
Miss Anderson:
Single room for full period (£6 per night).
Double room with bath available Feb 20-22 only (£12 per night).
Double room with shower (£11 per night) available Feb 23-25
Please ask if acceptable RP

2d

Write Jenny's reply to the letter in 2c.

2e

Write Mr Owen's reply, **accepting** or **refusing** the accommodation.

Harold meets Jenny in the college coffee bar.

HAROLD: Jen, some friends of mine down in Maidenhead have asked me down there the weekend after next. I was just wondering . . . would you like to come along too?

JENNY: Well, I don't know . . .

HAROLD: Oh, don't get any wrong ideas! They've got an enormous house. And they're great fun. They're planning some sort of party for the Saturday night.

JENNY: Well, it would be nice to get out of London, I suppose . . .

HAROLD: Yes, we all need a break. You'll come, then?

JENNY: Yes, I'd love to . . .

Use suitable information from the conversation in 3a to write the letter which Harold Lamb got from his friends in Maidenhead. Invent any suitable details (e.g. the name and address of the friends, the reason for the party) and mention that he can bring a friend.

Write Harold's reply.

4a

The following day, Jenny gets this letter from Andrew.

22 Peebles Road, Edinburgh.
14th Feb (!).

Darling Jenny,
I've just had a bright idea! Why don't I come down to London the weekend after next? I've got some friends in Camden Town who can put me up. I could come down on the Friday evening – then we could have the whole weekend together. It would be nice to go to a theatre on the Saturday.

I know this is very short notice, but

I do miss you terribly! Can you give me a ring and let me know if it's ok?
All my love,
Andrew.

 4b

Jenny rings up Andrew and says that she is not free that weekend. Andrew is very disappointed. Afterwards, she decides to write to him to make things clear.

Write Jenny's letter:
- explain that you have another boyfriend;
- say that you are not in love with him, but that you go out with him quite a lot;
- suggest that you and Andrew do not write to each other quite so often for a while.

 4c

Write Andrew's reply.

9. February-March

Diana Stone is determined to find another au pair girl. She goes to the Orme Agency.

MISS ORME: Of course, this isn't exactly an easy time of year to find an au pair, but if you're willing to accept someone just for the summer . . .

MRS STONE: Yes, that would be quite all right. Of course, I would have preferred . . .

MISS ORME: And you do live some way out of London. That's another small problem.

MRS STONE: There's an excellent train service, though, from Oxted to Victoria.

MISS ORME: All the same, a lot of girls do ask to be *in* London. However, I'm sure we can fix you up.

MRS STONE: What's the next move, then?

MISS ORME: Well, you have to fill in this form and, of course, there's a fee of £15 . . . Then I'll go through our list and contact you in a day or two.

Fill in this form which Miss Orme gives Diana Stone. Use information from the earlier units to help you.

```
ORME EMPLOYMENT AGENCY, 132 GLOUCESTER ROAD, LONDON SW7H 2HD.

PLEASE PRINT IN BLOCK CAPITALS
                                    DATE ..6. MARCH......
NAME ............................    TEL.NO: ..............
ADDRESS.....................................................

...........................................................
WHEN DO YOU WANT THE GIRL TO ARRIVE? .......................
HOW LONG DO YOU WANT HER TO STAY? MAXIMUM ..................
                                  MINIMUM ..................
WILL SHE HAVE HER OWN BEDROOM? .............................
WHAT WILL HER DUTIES BE? ...................................

...........................................................
DO YOU HAVE ANY OTHER DOMESTIC HELP? .......................
WHERE CAN SHE ATTEND ENGLISH CLASSES? ...................
HOW MANY HOURS A WEEK CAN SHE ATTEND ENGLISH CLASSES? 6 HOURS
WHICH DAY WILL SHE BE FREE EACH WEEK? .MONDAY..............
HOW MANY FREE EVENINGS WILL SHE HAVE? ......................
HOW MUCH POCKET MONEY WILL SHE GET? (£5-7 a week is recommended)
...........................................................
NATIONALITY OF FAMILY ............. HUSBAND'S JOB ..........
CHILDREN: BOYS ............... AGES ...... GIRLS .....AGES ....
          ................         .....         .....    ....
          ................         .....         .....    ....
HAVE YOU EVER HAD AN AU PAIR GIRL BEFORE?  IF SO, GIVE DETAILS
...........................................................
...........................................................
ANY OTHER INFORMATION ......................................
.............................. SIGNED ...................
```

2a

The following day, Miss Orme telephones Mrs Stone.

MISS ORME: Mrs Stone? Miss Orme from the agency here. I think I've found someone who might suit you.

MRS STONE: Oh, that's splendid. Can you tell me something about her?

MISS ORME: Well, her name's Helga Schmidt – she's German – from Freiburg, actually.

MRS STONE: And how old is she?

MISS ORME: Mm, let me see – she's 22. She seems a sensible sort of girl – on paper, at any rate. Very anxious to improve her English.

MRS STONE: And how soon could she come?

MISS ORME: Almost immediately, it seems. But I think at this stage it would be better if you wrote to her personally. Tell her something about yourself and your family. You can also find out anything else about her that you want to know. Now, I'll just give you her address . . .

2b

This is the letter which Diana Stone writes to Helga Schmidt.

> 26 Chestnut Drive,
> Oxted, Surrey
>
> Tel: Oxted 3971
>
> 7th March
>
> Dear Miss Schmidt,
>   I have just been given your name by the Orme Agency and they have asked me to get in touch with you directly.
>   I am sure you would like to know something about the family you are coming to.
>
> *Continue with appropriate information about the Stone family*
>
> Although Oxted is some way out of London, ————.
> So you won't find it difficult to ————.
>   There is one other thing. I really do need you here by the end of March, when Simon, Jane and Mark will be on holiday from school. Could you please let me know as soon as possible whether you can come by that time?
>   Looking forward to meeting you,
>   Yours sincerely,
>   Diana Stone.

This is the letter which Helga sends to Mrs Stone.

                                        FREIBURG,

                                        Marienstrasse 42.

                                        14th March 19--

Dear Mrs Stone,

    Thank you for your letter and for all the information you gave me about yourself and your family.

    I shall be very happy to come and work as an 'au pair' with you during the summer. I am also writing to the Orme Agency to confirm this.

    I regret, however, that I cannot come before ..... because ..... . I hope this is acceptable.

    I would like to ask you a favour. I am extremely anxious to make the best use of my short stay in England by improving my English. Could you please send me .....

Continue Helga's letter. Refer to 3a for details of her request.

                                With best wishes,

                                Helga Schmidt.

Write Helga Schmidt's letter to the Orme Agency confirming that she is going to work for the Stone family.

Scottish Tourist Board
333 Shaftesbury Avenue
London WIV 7DD

Tel: Ol 734 2555
Cables: SCOTOURLON

March 21.

Dear Helga,

My wife asked me to get some information about language schools for you. I don't know anything about these places myself, so I asked a friend for advice, & he suggested the names of these schools. Their brochures are enclosed. I do hope you will find one to suit you.

My wife and I are both looking forward to having you with us very soon — and so are the children.

With best wishes,

John Stone.

Helga chooses the Victoria Language and Secretarial College. Complete her application form. Use any information you know about Helga, and invent any other suitable details.

```
VICTORIA LANGUAGE AND SECRETARIAL COLLEGE,
25 VICTORIA STREET,  LONDON  SW1B 8HJ



Application for enrolment in a language course.

FAMILY NAME.................... FIRST NAME(S)...........

ADDRESS IN YOUR OWN COUNTRY............................

FATHER'S OCCUPATION............... YOUR OCCUPATION.......

DATE OF BIRTH.................NATIONALITY..............

ADDRESS IN ENGLAND....................................
......................................................

Which courses do you wish to attend? (Tick appropriate box)

9am - 12, Monday to Friday ☐     5pm - 7pm, Monday, Wednesday,
                                                   Friday ☐

1pm - 4pm, Monday to Friday ☐     5pm - 8pm, Tuesday and Thursday
                                                          ☐

All courses last 4 weeks.  Please tick the date you wish to
begin.

January 5    ☐     May  11  ☐     September  1   ☐
February 2   ☐     June  8  ☐     September 28   ☐
March  2     ☐     July  6  ☐     October 26     ☐
March 30     ☐     August 3 ☐     November 23    ☐

The college is closed for one week at Christmas and Easter.

IS THIS YOUR FIRST VISIT TO ENGLAND? ....................

IF NOT, GIVE DETAILS OF PREVIOUS VISITS..................
......................................................

WHERE HAVE YOU STUDIED ENGLISH?.........................

FOR HOW MANY YEARS?.....................................

HOW DID YOU HEAR ABOUT THIS COLLEGE?....................

SIGNATURE............................. DATE..............
```

Write the covering letter which Helga sends to the college with her application form.

10. May

Donald and Patsy are on holiday in Dubrovnik. They are sitting and having a drink in a cafe by the harbour.

PATSY: I hate to mention it on this lovely spring morning – but don't you think we should write a few letters to people back home?

DONALD: Oh, let's just send postcards . . .

PATSY: Well, that's all right for the girls, but I think Louise, at least, deserves a letter. She and Piero were very good to us in Bologna. And then there's Steve.

DONALD: Tell, you what. *You* write to Louise – I'm no good at thank-you letters, anyway. And I'll drop Steve a few lines.

PATSY: Well, OK. But don't be too hard on him, will you? He's been very good lately.

DONALD: Don't worry. And you'll see to the postcards for the girls, will you?

PATSY: OK. All you'll have to do is sign them!

DONALD: Fine. Well, I think that calls for another drink, don't you?

Hotel Place,
Dubrovnik,
10th May.

Dear Steve,
We got to Dubrovnik the day before yesterday — after a rather rough crossing from Ancona. Your mother was sea-sick of course!

Now continue.

Describe the hotel: just outside the city walls/marvellous view of the harbour/own beach for swimming/excellent food/eat outside most of the time.

Refer to the drive through Italy: saw several old friends in Bologna/spent day in Ravenna/Louise may visit Britain this summer.

I hope things are going well at school and that you are managing at home OK. Mum sends her love — and hopes your cooking is improving!

Love,
Dad.

(1c)

Write the letter Patsy sends to Louise. Thank her for her hospitality and say how much you enjoyed your stay there (+ reasons). Talk about the hotel you are staying at in Dubrovnik. Say how much you are looking forward to seeing her in the summer, etc. Refer to 1b for any suitable information.

(1d)

Write the postcard which Patsy sends to Judy and Jenny.

2a

A couple of days later, Donald Anderson is reading an English newspaper.

DONALD: Patsy! Just take a look at this!

STUDENT PROTEST

STUDENTS at the Walter Scott High School, Edinburgh, continued to demonstrate this week for more participation in school management.

A spokesman for the students, 17 year old Stephen Anderson, has declared: 'If necessary, we will go on strike! We have absolutely no say in the running of our school. It's not democratic. At 18 we have the right to vote, but at school we are treated like children!'

The school authorities are considering what action to take against the students.

PATSY: The paper's three days old. What do you think we should do? Phone Steve?

DONALD: Well, it might be better to send a telegram to Judy. She'll know all about it. If it's really serious, perhaps we should go home.

 2b

Write the telegram message Patsy sends to Judy. Ask for the latest details of the situation at Stephen's school and whether she thinks they should come home early.

 2c

Write the telegram Judy sends in reply.

The Andersons are back in Edinburgh.

DONALD: Well frankly, Steve, I think you were very lucky. You might have been expelled – and then what?

STEVE: You don't understand, Dad. We simply had to do something.

DONALD: Well, you don't have to threaten to go on strike. That's serious.

STEVE: It's the only language they understand. Now, at least, they know what we think.

PATSY: Come on, Don. They can't go on treating students like children.

DONALD: Oh, you always take Steve's side. Anyway, how am I going to answer this letter from Steve's headmaster? He blames Steve for most of what happened. He says he persuaded the other students to join in the demonstration.

STEVE: Well, that's just *his* point of view.

PATSY: You just leave the letter to me. *I'll* write to Mr Perkins. After all, students do have some rights, you know, and I think I shall say so in my letter.

Write the letter which Patsy Anderson sends to Steve's headmaster:

– apologise for the way in which school life was disrupted by the demonstration;
– point out that many of the school rules are old-fashioned and are not suitable for young people today;
– add any other ideas of your own.

Write the letter Steve sends to Harm. Invent appropriate details.

11. June–July

Helga has been with the Stones for about six weeks.

HELGA: Oh, Mrs Stone . . . I was just wondering . . . Can I have Tuesday off instead of Monday?
Tuesday? No, I'm afraid not. I have my St. John's Ambulance class that evening. And someone has to look after the children.

HELGA: But it's the only day I can see Harold. It's his *one* free day. On other evenings, he has classes.

MRS STONE: Well, I can't help that. After all, you didn't come here just to find a boyfriend, did you?

HELGA: I know – but he does help me with my English. He's a teacher, you know.

MRS STONE: Hm.

HELGA: Well, if you won't let me have Tuesday off, I'll just have to stay out later in the evenings.

MRS STONE: That's your affair, I suppose. Provided it doesn't interfere with your work, of course.

This is the letter which Helga writes to an English girl, Helen Scott, who is an au pair in Freiburg with some friends of Helga's family.

```
                                        Oxted.

                                        2nd June.


Dear Helen,

    I'm sorry I haven't written to you before, but I've been very
busy.  I hope you are still enjoying life in Freiburg.

    I must say, you are lucky to be with such a nice family.  I wish
I could say the same about the Stones!  He's quite pleasant .....
```

Continue the paragraph. Refer to what you know about the Stones, and to the conversation in 1a. Invent any other suitable details.

```
    However, one nice thing has happened.  I've got to know a very
nice boy here.  He's a teacher at the language school I go to .....
```

Continue the paragraph, inventing any appropriate details.

```
                            Hope to hear from you soon,

                                    Best wishes
                                    Helga
```

The Stone's telephone rings in the middle of the night.

HELGA: Mr Stone! . . . It's me, Helga.

MR STONE: Helga! What on earth has happened to you? It's nearly 1.30!

HELGA: Well, you see, I've been in a car crash.

MR STONE: Are you badly hurt?

HELGA: Well, I've broken my arm – and I've got a few cuts and bruises.

MR STONE: So are they keeping you in hospital?

HELGA: No, that's just the point. They say they can't find a bed for me, and they want you to come and get me.

MR STONE: At *this* hour! Where are you, anyway?

HELGA: Croydon General Hospital.

MR STONE: God, it'll take ages! Oh, all right . . . tell them I'll be there as soon as I can.

After Helga's accident, Diana Stone writes to the Orme Agency.

26 Chestnut Drive,
Oxted, Surrey

Tel: Oxted 3971

14th June.

Dear Miss Orme,

I spoke to you last week concerning Miss Helga Schmidt, who came to me as an au pair through your agency.

I promised at the time to be patient with her because of her broken arm, and I would like to say that I have continued to treat her with the greatest sympathy.

However, this does not solve the problem. The fact is, Miss Schmidt is no longer a <u>help</u> to us, but a <u>hindrance</u>. She is able to look after herself — which infact she does very well! — but she is absolutely no use to me either in the house or with the children. I am sure she <u>could</u> be, if she made more effort, but in my opinion, she is simply taking advantage of the situation.

In the circumstances, I must ask you to find me a new girl. I shall in any case ask Miss Schmidt to return to Germany as soon as possible.

Yours sincerely,

Diana Stone.

Diana Stone tells Helga that she has complained to the Agency, and that she wants her to go back to Germany. Helga is furious and decides to write to the Agency herself. Write Helga's letter. Say that you are doing your best, but that Mrs Stone is most unsympathetic. Ask the Agency to find you another job because you want to stay in England.

4a

Jenny has gone to visit Harold in his flat.

JENNY: Sounds to me as if you were lucky to escape with just a broken leg!

HAROLD: Well, I wasn't going very fast. Only about 25 miles an hour. But if I hadn't swerved, the other car would have hit me. He was on the wrong side of the road, the bloody fool!

JENNY: You didn't get his number, of course?

HAROLD: No such luck! All I remember, it was a white MG. Then I hit the lamp-post. The front of the car's completely smashed in. About four hundred pounds' worth of damage, the garage says.

JENNY: It's lucky you were alone! The other person might have been killed.

HAROLD: Hm, that's true . . . Well, I suppose I'd better fill in this insurance claim.

JENNY: Well, in that case, I'll get on with another of these job applications. I haven't heard a thing from Impex – those people I had an interview with last week. Don't suppose I'll get the job, anyway . . .

4b

Complete Harold Lamb's Accident Claim Form. Refer to the conversation in 4a for appropriate information, and invent any other details. See Unit 12, 1a for Harold's address.

Accident Report Form

Driver of Vehicle

Full name ....

Address ....

Occupation.. Date of Birth ....

Driving Licence No: **LAMB/212069/DP9DF**

How long has the driver held the licence? ....

Vehicle

Registration No: .... Make ....

Year of make ....

Is the vehicle owned by the insured? ....

Is the vehicle registered in his name? ....

Precise use at the time of the accident? ....

State damage to vehicle ....

Name and address of garage where vehicle will be repaired ....

Is the vehicle at the garage now? ....

If not, when will it be taken? ....

Accident

Date .... Time ....

Place .... Town ....

Own speed .... Width of road ....

Road and weather conditions ....

Was the accident reported to the police? ....

Name of police officer ....

Here are two job advertisements which Jenny has seen.

> **PERSONAL SECRETARY** to architect in busy London office. 10-6 plus some Saturdays. Good typing essential. Excellent salary for the right applicant. Send application to Mary Hall Agency, 24 St. James St., W1, quoting ref: T/375.

> **DO YOU HAVE A GOOD SENSE OF HUMOUR?** I'm leaving my present boss to get married, and whoever takes him on will certainly need one! However, the pay is good, the office comfortable, and the people pleasant. You must have good typing and shorthand, and one foreign language would be an advantage. Plus a good telephone manner and appearance. Apply to: Ann Mills, EFD Exports Ltd., 35 Chancery Lane, London WC1.

Choose one of these jobs and write Jenny's letter of application for it. Use the information you know about her from earlier conversations and letters.

5

Later that afternoon, the doorbell rings. Jenny opens the door.

HELGA: Oh, hullo. I'm Helga . . . is Harold in?

JENNY: Yes . . . er, do come in . . .

HAROLD: Helga! I wasn't expecting you! Jenny . . . er . . . this is . . . um . . . Helga Schmidt. Jenny Anderson.

HELGA: How do you do?

JENNY: How do you do? . . . Oh, you've hurt your arm!

HELGA: Yes. Didn't Harold tell you? I was in the car accident with him last week . . .

12. June

1a

This is the letter that Jenny gets from Harold Lamb.

Flat 27, Jubilee Mansions, Battersea Park Road, London SW 14
                                                    June 17

Dear Jen,

   I am very sorry about what happened yesterday. I wanted to tell you about
Helga before, but somehow I could never find the right moment. And then she
walked in like that! It gave me a shock too.

   I was quite serious about you until recently. Then I met Helga and everything changed overnight. I think I'm really in love with her.

   Please forgive me, Jen. You really are one of the nicest girls I know, and
I hope we can continue to be good friends.

Much love,

Harold

1b

Write Jenny's reply.

1c

This is the letter Jenny gets from Andrew.

> 22 Peebles Road, Edinburgh.
> 20th June.
>
> Dearest Jenny, Do you know how long it is
> since we last wrote to each other? Over
> 2 months! I know we agreed not to write
> to each other quite so much – but it's a pity
> we stopped writing altogether. Of course, being
> so far apart didn't help the situation.
>   Anyway, I just wanted to let you know
> that I still think about you & care for
> you. If you're coming to Edinburgh this
> summer, I hope we can meet. I mean,
> can we? or have things changed too
> much?
>   I've just about finished with exams. How
> did yours go? Have you started looking
> round for jobs yet? Do write.
>   As ever,
>   Andrew.

1d

Write Jenny's reply.

This is the letter which Jenny gets from the firm she had an interview with (see Unit 11, 4a).

---

impex ltd

55 Knightsbridge
London SW7B 5BX

Telephone: 01 584 5555
Cables: IMPEX
Telex: 63974 IMP

Date: 24.6.--   Ref: 42/6/S   1f/JRS

Dear Miss Anderson,

   I must apologise for having taken so long to give you the results of the interview you had with us on June 10. As you are aware, however, there were many applicants for the post and we wanted to consider each one carefully.

   I regret that we are unable to offer you the position you applied for at our London office. There is, however, an unexpected vacancy in our Rome branch, where our receptionist has just resigned in order to get married. I need hardly say that this is a responsible job, but we feel sure that with your experience of living in Italy, and your knowledge of the language, you will be well suited to it.

   The contract would initially be for one year, starting on September 1. I cannot at present give you exact details of salary or terms of employment, but I think you will find them attractive.

   Could you please let me know as soon as possible if you are interested in this position.

                              Yours sincerely,

                              JRS.

                              Julius R. Slobin,
                              <u>Personnel Manager</u>

Miss J. Anderson,
16, Upper Street,
LONDON N1.

Write Jenny's reply.

This is the letter that Helga gets from Harold Lamb.

Flat 27, Jubilee Mansions, Battersea Park Road, London SW14

June 17

Darling Helga,

Whenever I ring up, that awful Stone woman always answers the phone and says that you are too busy to come and speak to me. I don't know if this is true - but I just hope you aren't annoyed with me.

Look, that girl you met at my flat - Jenny Anderson - she was just an old friend who happened to drop in to say hullo. I have been out with her a couple of times, but there has never been anything between us.

You mean a lot to me, Helga. I've never told you, but I think I'm in love with you. In fact, I'd like to marry you. Please let me know how you feel.

Best love, my darling. I'm <u>longing</u> to hear from you.

Harold

Write Helga's reply.

This is the letter which Helga gets from the Orme Agency.

ORME EMPLOYMENT AGENCY

132 Gloucester Road,
London SW7H 2HD

Tel: 01 589 7243

June 21st 19--

Dear Miss Schmidt,

We are sorry that things have not worked out well between you and your present employer, Mrs D. Stone. Without blaming anyone for the situation, we agree that you cannot continue in your present employment, but at the same time we should be sorry if you had to return to Germany.

We wonder if you would be interested in a rather different sort of job - as a companion to two old ladies who live in Yorkshire. Your duties would be very light, (which means that your injury would be no disadvantage) and you would have plenty of time to continue with your language studies. One of the ladies has even offered to help you.

I look forward to hearing from you about this proposal.

Yours sincerely,

Mirabel Orme

Mirabel Orme (Miss)

Miss Helga Schmidt,
c/o Mrs Diana Stone,
26 Chestnut Avenue,
Oxted,
Surrey.

2d

Write Helga's reply.

3a

David gets this letter from Canada.

The Festival Theatre,
Toronto, Canada
Tel: 416 723819

Ref: 78/4/UK

28 June 19--

David Cameron,
16 Upper Street,
LONDON N1,
England.

Dear Mr Cameron,

    Our Casting Director, James Burgess, has been in touch
with the major London theatrical agents prior to his visit
to Britain in July and August. Your agent, Marcia Lang,
has recommended you to us as a result of your success in
the BBC television version of <u>Twelfth Night</u>.

    We wonder whether, in principle, you would be interested
in joining our company next season. We shall be presenting
four classical plays between March and October: <u>Twelfth
Night</u>, <u>The Duchess of Malfi</u>, <u>The School for Scandal</u> and
<u>Hedda Gabler</u>.

    Although the season only runs for six months, there is
a two month rehearsal period first. You would therefore
have to join us by January 1. The salary would be in the
range $ Canadian 1500 to 1800p.m. and accommodation would
be provided (if you are unmarried).

    Perhaps you would write and let us know whether you are
interested in coming to Canada. If so, we will arrange for
you to meet James Burgess when he is in London in mid-July.

                  Yours sincerely,

V. Newsham

              Virginia Newsham,
       <u>Secretary to the Casting Director</u>

pr/VN

3b

David and Judy discuss the **advantages** and **disadvantages** of going to Canada. In the
light of their decision, write David's reply to Virginia Newsham.

3c

Write Judy's letter to her mother, telling her about the offer from Toronto and what
they have decided to do.

3d

Write Patsy's reply.

4a

Patsy gets this letter from the magazine editor.

---

and People Places

178 Greengate   Manchester 20H 6B
Tel: 061 834 9898

July 15 19--   Ref: 79/8/K

Dear Mrs Anderson,

I am writing with reference to your series of stories on hospital
life which we published earlier this year under the title Backwards
and Forwards.

These have attracted the attention of Frederick Featherstone, who is
Programme Controller (Drama) of ANT (Associated Northern Television).
He has written to say how impressed he was with the stories and how
he would like to base a television series on them.

I think I should warn you exactly what this means. Since you have
had no experience of writing for television, he will naturally want
to use his own scriptwriter, and will merely make use of your ideas
and characters. However, the fee paid for the use of your stories is
likely to be substantial.

Would you please write directly to Mr Featherstone informing him of
your decision, and send a copy of your letter to me. His address is:

                    Frederick Featherstone,
                    Programme Controller (Drama),
                    ANT,
                    95 Kirkgate,
                    Leeds 2YR 7KP,
                    Yorkshire.

With my best wishes and congratulations,
Yours sincerely,

Arnold Jackson

Arnold Jackson   rf/AJ
Editor

Mrs Patsy Anderson,
18 Craigmillar Road,
Edinburgh EG6 7YY,
Scotland.

4b

Write Patsy's letter to Frederick Featherstone.

4c

Donald Anderson is in the United States on business. Write Patsy's letter to him. Refer
both to her own TV offer and to David's letter from Toronto.

4d

Write Donald's reply.

5a

John Stone is also in the United States with Donald Anderson on a business trip. At the end of it, he is invited to stay with an American colleague. This is the telegram he sends Diana.

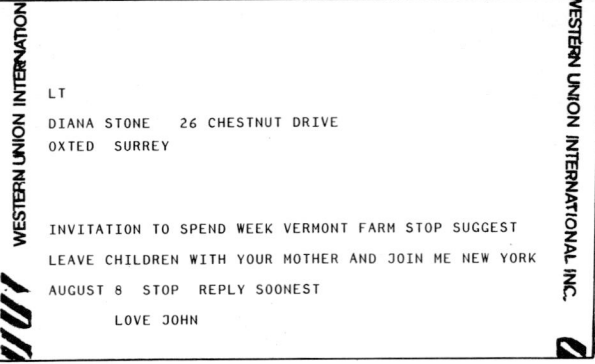

```
WESTERN UNION INTERNATIONAL                           WESTERN UNION INTERNATIONAL INC.

          LT
          DIANA STONE    26 CHESTNUT DRIVE
          OXTED   SURREY


          INVITATION TO SPEND WEEK VERMONT FARM STOP SUGGEST
          LEAVE CHILDREN WITH YOUR MOTHER AND JOIN ME NEW YORK
          AUGUST 8  STOP  REPLY SOONEST
                LOVE JOHN
```

5b

Write the telegram Diana sends in reply.

6a

This is a letter Steve gets from Harm.

> De Wittemkade 149,
> AMSTERDAM W.
> July 17th.
>
> Dear Steve,
> Some good news for you ! You remember you were keen on coming across
> here this summer with your group? Well - I've just had a call from
> Piet de Louwer, who is putting on a show called 'Sounds International'
> at the Youth Festival which they are holding at the Cultureel Centrum
> in Amstelveen (just outside Amsterdam).   It's in the first week of
> September.
>
> He's absolutely desperate because the English group he invited have
> just backed out (they got a more attractive offer from the States).
> So I mentioned your name.   Of course he had heard of you - you're
> famous over here because of all the publicity you got from that
> school demonstration ! - and he said: Yes, get him over here!!!
>
> There's just one small snag: no fees and no expenses. But I can put
> you up, and I'm pretty sure I can find somewhere for the others to
> sleep.   So it's mainly fares and spending money.
>
> How about it?   It's going to be a good festival.   Write as soon as
> possible.
>
>   Yours
>   Harm

6b

Steve discusses this with Patsy, as Donald is still in the States. Write his reply to Harm.

THE CHARACTERS IN THE BOOK

Donald Anderson

Patsy Anderson

Jenny Anderson

Stephen Anderson

1. Donald Anderson, 46. Married to an American. Three children. Works for the Scottish Tourist Board in Edinburgh. Is trying to work out a new policy for the Scottish tourist industry, so makes frequent business trips abroad. Often visits his sister Louise, who is married to an Italian. 18 CRAIGMILLAR ROAD, EDINBURGH, EG6 7YY, SCOTLAND.

2. Patsy Anderson, 43. Donald's wife. Has just begun work as ward receptionist at one of the Edinburgh hospitals. Enjoys writing and keeps a diary. Is fairly progressive and usually supports Steve (see below) in his arguments with his father. She and Donald get on very well, however.

3. Jenny Anderson, 19. The Andersons' younger daughter. Has just spent a year in Bologna learning Italian. Is now beginning a year's secretarial course in London, where she lives with her married sister – an arrangement they both dislike. Has a boyfriend in Edinburgh, Andrew Buchan. FLAT B, 16 UPPER STREET, LONDON N1. TEL: 01-359 0507.

4. Stephen Anderson (Steve), 17. In his last year at school – which he does not enjoy much. Leader of a pop group which is beginning to be quite successful. The time he spends with this makes his father angry. Gets on well with his mother and his elder sister. Confides many of his problems in his Dutch penfriend, Harm Reinders (see page 64).

5. Judy Cameron, 22. The Andersons' elder daughter. Married to a young actor, David, with a baby, Nicholas. They live in a flat in North London. Before the baby was born, Judy studied jewellery at art school. She now works at home and sells her work. This provides just enough money for them to live on. Jenny and she argue a lot.

6. David Luis Cameron, 25. An Anglo-Argentinian who studied acting at a London theatre school. Has had a few small parts in plays and on TV, but nothing big. His agent, Marcia Lang, is helping him to find work. Meanwhile, he relies on Judy's income from her jewellery to support the family.

7. John Stone, 32. Works in the London office of the Scottish Tourist Board and is responsible for keeping in touch with Tourist Boards in other countries. Goes on business trips with Donald Anderson. Is married and has 3 children: Jane, Simon and Mark. Lives outside London – about 40 minutes. 26 CHESTNUT DRIVE, OXTED, SURREY.

8. Diana Stone, 31. John's wife. Very discontented and dislikes being tied to the house and children. Usually has an 'au pair' girl to help her, but she is so unpleasant to them that they never stay long! Belongs to a lot of women's organisations.

Continued on page 64

Judy Cameron

David Luis Cameron

John Stone

Diana Stone

Anne-Marie Mignen

Helga Schmidt

Harold Lamb

Andrew Buchan

Harm Reinders

Louise Donatini

Mirabel Orme

Sheila Sinclair

Ros Winter

Jean Andrews

9. **Anne-Marie Mignen, 19.** A French girl from Nantes who spends some time as an 'au pair' with the Stones. She leaves when she is told she will have to look after the children on her own.

10. **Helga Schmidt, 22.** A university student from Freiburg, Southern Germany. Comes to the Stones as an 'au pair' and attends English classes at the college where Harold Lamb (see below) teaches. Is strong-willed, and does not get on well with Mrs Stone.

11. **Harold Lamb, 30.** Teacher of English to foreign students at the Victoria Language and Secretarial College, where Jenny Anderson and Helga Schmidt are students. Goes out with both of them. Lives in a flat in a large block in South London.
FLAT 27, JUBILEE MANSIONS, BATTERSEA PARK ROAD, LONDON SW14.

12. **Andrew Buchan, 20.** A student at Edinburgh University. Jenny's boyfriend until she goes to London.
22 PEEBLES ROAD, EDINBURGH.

13. **Harm Reinders, 19.** A student at Amsterdam University. Has stayed several times with the Andersons in Edinburgh, and has been Steve's penfriend for many years.
DE WITTEMKADE 149, AMSTERDAM W, NETHERLANDS.

14. **Louise Donatini, 40.** Donald Anderson's sister. Married to an Italian, Piero, in Bologna.

15. **Mirabel Orme, 55.** Runs the Orme Agency for 'au pair' girls.

16. **Sheila Sinclair, 24.** Donald Anderson's secretary.

17. **Ros Winter, 20.** A friend of Jenny's at the secretarial college.

18. **Jean Andrews, 35.** A friend of Patsy Anderson's.

LONGMAN GROUP LIMITED
London

Associated companies, branches and representatives throughout the world

© Longman Group Ltd. 1978

First published 1978
Second impression 1980

ISBN 0 582 79100 6

Acknowledgements:
Derek Collard for page 29; Yugoslav Tourist Board for page 47.

Printed in Great Britain at
The Pitman Press, Bath